WHERE'S MOM?

WHERE'S MOM?

The High Calling of Wives and Mothers

DOROTHY KELLEY PATTERSON

Foreword by
Dennis Rainey

CROSSWAY BOOKS

A DIVISION OF
GOOD NEWS PUBLISHERS
WHEATON, ILLINOIS

Where's Mom?

Published by Crossway Books
    a division of Good News Publishers
    1300 Crescent Street
    Wheaton, Illinois 60187

Adapted from a chapter in *Recovering Biblical Manhood and Womanhood*, edited by Wayne Grudem and John Piper (Crossway Books, 1991).

The Council on Biblical Manhood and Womanhood was established in 1987 for the purpose of studying and setting forth biblical teachings on the relationship between men and women, especially in the home and the church.

Cover design: David LaPlaca

Cover photo: Wood River Gallery

First printing 2003

Printed in the United States of America

Library of Congress Cataloging-in-Publication Data
Patterson, Dorothy Kelley, 1943-
    Where's mom? : the high calling of wives and mothers / Dorothy
Kelley Patterson.
        p. cm.
    Adapted from a chapter in Recovering biblical manhood and
womanhood / edited by Wayne Grudem and John Piper. 1991.
    Includes bibliographical references.
    ISBN 1-58134-534-8 (alk. paper)
    1. Christian women—Religious life. 2. Women—Biblical teaching.
I. Recovering biblical manhood and womanhood. II. Title.
BV4527.P386   2003
248.8'431—dc21   2003004144

CH		13	12	11	10	09	08	07	06	05	04	03
15	14	13	12	11	10	9	8	7	6	5	4	3	2	1

To special Mothers in my life:

DORIS WEISIGER KELLEY, who gave me life and reared me in the Lord

HONEY PATTERSON, who gave me an example of linking maternity and ministry by rearing my husband, Paige—a godly man without peer

RACHEL CORINE QUINLIN PATTERSON, who as the wife of my firstborn, Armour, may also someday be the mother of more grandchildren for me

CARMEN LEIGH PATTERSON HOWELL, who—at the encouragement of my son-in-love Mark—has made mothering a top priority and focus

ABIGAIL LEIGH and REBEKAH ELIZABETH HOWELL, who will grow into womanhood and perhaps usher in yet another generation by giving me great-grandchildren

KATHLEEN KELLEY, who, as a surrogate mother, pours love and affection on every child who comes into her elementary school library

CHARLENE SUE KELLEY KAEMMERLING, who has emptied her energies and creativity into the rearing of Beth, Angie, Kelley, Perry, and Claire

RHONDA HARRINGTON KELLEY, who, as First Lady of New Orleans Baptist Theological Seminary, gives herself in sacrificial service to students and families and to mentoring women throughout the world

EILEEN MARIE KELLEY TURRENTINE, who chose her daughter Sarah and drew her to heart and hearth

RIMA AMAD, who has lovingly borne and on a distant shore reared my niece Nadia and nephew Yaser

Contents

Foreword

One of the people I admire the most is Dorothy Patterson. She is a courageous patriot for the family. For more than forty years she made her own marriage and family a priority, and she has spent more than three decades of her life equipping others to be successful in their homes.

Increasingly, we live in an age that depreciates and demeans motherhood. As a result, we have a generation of mothers and children who have suffered much. In her book *Where's Mom?* Dorothy explores the high and holy calling of being a wife and a mother. Her writings are persuasive, and her illustrations are conclusive: *Mothers matter*.

During the last thirty years, our nation has languished in the midst of a feminist social experiment with the family. But feminism has failed. It has not delivered on its promises to women of self-actualization and fulfillment. Instead it has brought women more suffering, more confusion, and more restlessness than ever before.

In the wake of feminism's failure, Dorothy offers a clear and compelling biblical pattern for wives and mothers. If there has ever been a day when this book was needed, it is today. My prayer is that God will use this book to raise up a generation of women and men who esteem, value, and honor one of life's most noble and high callings—motherhood.

Dennis Rainey,
President, FamilyLife

1

Is Homemaking a Job?

Upon completion of our graduate work in theology at New Orleans Baptist Theological Seminary in 1970, my husband, Paige, and I moved with our two children to Fayetteville, Arkansas. My husband assumed the pastorate of the First Baptist Church of Fayetteville, and I continued my role as his helper—but with some major adjustments.

First, the responsibility of caring for a premature infant "crying machine," added to the already arduous task of keeping up with a card-carrying member of the "Terrible Twos' Society," was a life-changing jolt to the efficient routine I had of working as a highly paid executive secretary by day and amusing a drop-in toddler at night.

Second, my weekend responsibilities as a pastor's wife in New Orleans, which I had previously fulfilled as a mere addendum to my role as a "professional woman," were certainly not from the script that had been presented to me upon our arrival in Fayetteville. There I was to play the part of a young wife, following the steps of an older and highly experienced pastor's wife who had enjoyed star billing in the community as well as the church for many years and whose wardrobe did not take into account two babies!

Third, the intellectually stimulating and mind-stretching dialogue of a theological community definitely overshadowed the dissonant and monosyllabic monologue of a frenzied mother whose only moments for reflection came within the confines of the bathroom—and that only if she managed to enter the room alone, which was a feat in itself!

Confused and frustrated, I wondered if this season, too, really would pass and if indeed it passed, whether I also would be passed by forever—at least as far as making any worthwhile contribution to society. During my seminary days I had maintained a rigorous schedule as a full-time student, studying both Hebrew and Greek, coupled with multiple part-time jobs and the unending responsibilities of a pastor's wife. After completing my master's degree, I entered motherhood and moved to a full-time job while my husband completed his doctoral work. Although I pursued motherhood as enthusiastically as I had every other adventure in my life—I even breast-fed my son for thirteen months while working full time—I can see in looking back that my first and freshest energies, not to mention the most productive part of my day, were devoted to professional pursuits away from home.

When my family moved to Arkansas, I quickly became aware of a void in my life. My theological training seemed a waste in preparing me for the task of motherhood. In the midst of this frustrating time, I turned to the Lord. I determined to read through the Bible systematically with a new purpose in my daily quiet time: I committed myself to finding God's message for me personally as a woman, as a wife, and as a mother. This experience became the catalyst for my life and ministry. From it came "The Bible Speaks on Being a Woman," a series of messages that I have been sharing with women through the years.

My life and goals and perspective were forever changed. In

every single book of the Bible, I found that God had a word for me. That word was not always comforting; in fact, sometimes it was like a sword to my heart; but always I knew that it was authoritative and, if authoritative, true, regardless of culture, circumstances, or perceived relevance. I came to realize that God did not expect me to determine how to adapt His Word to my situation. Instead, He expected me to mold myself according to the consistent and clear principles found in His Word. God did not expect me to interpret His principles in light of my gifts and intellect, but He admonished me, including my gifts and intellect and creativity, "to be conformed to the image of his Son" (Rom. 8:29).[1]

Even at this juncture as I enter my senior years, God is not waiting for me to determine what directives are relevant for me as a twenty-first-century American woman, but He is making clear throughout Scripture His demand for my absolute obedience, even willing submission in the Spirit of Christ Himself, who said, "I desire to do your will, O my God" (Ps. 40:8).

Consequently, even in those early years of motherhood, my chosen role of wife and mother took on new significance; I viewed my extensive academic preparation and professional experience in a new light; my commitment to marriage and home gained an added dimension—a divine covenant relationship reaching beyond a contractual agreement between my husband and me to include the Creator God Himself, who said, "What therefore God has joined together, let not man separate" (Matt. 19:6).

Bearing a new liberated identity, many women—even those who are committed evangelicals—have devoted themselves to ambitious busyness everywhere but in the home. They are enmeshed in overwhelming volunteerism, either consciously or subconsciously working to achieve accolades and recognition in the community; or they are half-hearted wives and mothers dedicated to hatching professional pursuits that promise powerful positions and pocketbook rewards. The biblical model that honors the keeping of the home, the helping of your husband, and the nurturing of your children is considered obsolete. Instead of encouraging adolescents to cut the apron strings from mother and venture out into society, now mothers are being begged not to cut the apron strings on their babies and catapult them prematurely into a menacing world! Mom and hot apple pie have been replaced by day care in institutional centers and cold apple turnovers at McDonald's!

Women have been liberated right out of the genuine freedom they have enjoyed to oversee the home, rear their children, and pursue personal creativity throughout the generations; they have been brainwashed to believe that the absence of a titled, payroll occupation enslaves a woman to failure, boredom, and imprisonment within the confines of the home. Although feminism speaks of liberation, self-fulfillment, personal rights, and breaking down barriers, these phrases inevitably mean the opposite.[2] In fact, the opposite is true because a salaried job and titled position can inhibit a woman's natural nesting instinct and maternity by inverting her priorities so that failures almost inevitably come in the rearing of her own children and the fashioning of an earthly shelter for those she loves most. The mundane accompanies every task, however high paying or prestigious the job, so that escape from boredom is not inevitable just because the workplace is not at home. And where is the time for personal creativity when she is in essence working two jobs—one at home and one away?

In the quest to be *all* you are meant to be, you must not forget *what* you are meant to be! The question has never been whether or not a woman wants the best for her husband and children and even for herself. Rather the real question is this: Is being someone's wife and another's mother really worth the investment of a life? Are the preparation of skills, the concentration of energies, and the commitment of both necessary to keep a home? The secular presuppositions of the present age, as well as your own assumptions and priorities, must continually be tested against the sure written Word of God, which warns, ". . . but test the spirits to see whether they are from God, for many false prophets have gone out into the world" (1 John 4:1).

Scripture contains *timeless and unchanging principles* that are to be the bedrock and foundation for living the Christian life—whether in the days of Abraham or in the twenty-first century in which we now live. Scripture also guides those who seek to unlock its treasure through *timely and changing applications* of those principles for every generation throughout history until the present day and even until the Lord returns.

QUESTIONS FOR REVIEW AND CONTEMPLATION

1. Profile your idea of the modern-day homemaker.
2. Compare biblical guidelines for homemaking with contemporary practices and discuss whether these are to be reconciled. If so, how?
3. Consider in your own life how to separate unchanging bedrock principles from changing cultural applications, especially as concerns what the Bible says about your role as a woman in your home.
4. What are the rewards for a woman who devotes her primary energies to her home and family?

SCRIPTURES TO STUDY

Genesis 1:27-31; 2:8-25

2

Is Homemaking a Challenging Career?

Over the long haul a career or professional pursuit requires training and preparation as well as commitment and dedication; it demands consistent activity and progressive advancement; it is a combination of training and preparation, commitment and loyalty, energy and time, excellence and achievement. Finding an efficient, capable person who is professionally adequate in many and varied careers simultaneously is rare indeed.

For example, would you want your family physician to be your postman and policeman as well? I doubt it. Why? Because you want him to specialize and sharpen his expertise in medicine. Yet you are certainly aware that your doctor dictates letters and reports and that he may on occasion sit down with a troubled patient as counselor. Within most careers a diversity of opportunity is never meant to cause the neglect of the priority responsibility. If the doctor gives the most productive part of his day to reports or counseling sessions, and if accordingly he neglects updating his professional skills and treats patients haphazardly, the doctor will soon have no need to make reports or do counseling because his patient load will dwindle. In other words, there is specialization in purpose and preparation but generalization in service and opportunity.

Homemaking in a sense is a career. Most dictionaries define the homemaker as "one who manages a household, especially a wife and mother." There are reasons why I believe this career is important enough to demand a woman's diligent preparation, foremost commitment, full energies, and greatest creativity. A homemaker does her job without the enticement of a paycheck, but she cannot be duplicated for any amount of money, for "She is far more precious than jewels" (Prov. 31:10). Dorothy Morrison wrote, "Homemaking is not employment for slothful, unimaginative, incapable women. It has as much challenge and opportunity, success and failure, growth and expansion, perks and incentives, as any corporate career."[3]

HOMEMAKING—A DIVINE ASSIGNMENT

For the wife, God's assignment is keeping the home—even down to changing the sheets, doing the laundry, and scrubbing the floors. In Titus 2:3-5, Paul admonishes the older women to teach the younger women, among other things, "to love their husbands and children . . . working at home" (oikourgous, Greek, literally "home-workers"). The home was once described as ". . . a place apart, a walled garden, in which certain virtues too easily crushed by modern life could be preserved," and the mother in this home was described as "The Angel in the House."[4] A 2003 Gallup poll showed that 96 percent of its respondents on a nine-point scale assigned top priority to the importance of family life. Families and health were rated as more important than money.[5]

Few women realize what great service they are doing for mankind and for the kingdom of Christ when they pour their energies into maintaining a shelter for the family and nurturing their children—the foundation on which all else is built. A mother builds something far more magnificent than any cathedral—i.e., the dwelling place for an immortal soul (both her child's fleshly tabernacle and his earthly abode). No professional pursuit so uniquely combines the most menial tasks with the most meaningful opportunities.

For me the book of Proverbs is the most practical book in the Bible. No other book is more saturated with home and family and the relationships therein. No other book has any more to say specifically to women.

Proverbs 31 contains a full-length portrait of a godly heroine finished in minute detail. Although passing to us through King Lemuel, the portrait of this godly woman, inspired by the Holy Spirit, came to the king from his mother (Prov. 31:1). The passage is significant not only for what it includes but also for what it omits. There is no mention of seeking personal rights or pursuing self-serving interests; neither is this woman's husband assigned to domestic pursuits. In fact, his occupation with other tasks is clearly stated: "The heart of her husband trusts in her. . . . Her husband is known in the gates when he sits among the elders of the land" (Prov. 31:11, 23).

This description of God's "Wonder Woman" is often labeled an "Alphabetic Ode," "The Golden ABC's of the Perfect Wife," "The Portrait of the Wife of Many Parts," or "A Paradigm for Brides-to-Be." Written as an acrostic, the first word of each verse of this beautiful and perfect ode of praise to womanhood begins with one of the twenty-two successive letters of the Hebrew alphabet. Perhaps its literary form is designed to make the passage easier to commit to memory, or its acrostic style may be a device used to emphasize that these characteristics describe God's ideal woman—upright and God-fearing woman of strength, committed homemaker, chaste helpmeet.

Although no woman can match skills and creativity perfectly with this model, each can identify her respective talents within the composite, and each can strive for the spiritual excellence of this woman of strength. This passage is recited in many Jewish homes during the family dinner on the eve of Sabbath, not only setting the high challenge for wife and mother but also expressing gratitude for her awesome service to the household.[6]

At least half of Proverbs 31:10-31 is occupied with the personal and domestic energy expended by this amazing woman. The New Testament, too, is clear in its emphasis on the energy and efficiency a woman needs to manage her household (Titus 2:5; 1 Tim. 2:10; 5:14). When Jesus reprimanded Martha, He did not condemn the vital housework she was doing; neither did He decry the gracious hospitality He Himself enjoyed from Martha's attention to His needs. Jesus did not say Martha's work at home was unnecessary, but He did admonish her not to be encumbered or burdened by her work to the *exclusion* of spiritual sustenance, which her sister Mary had so faithfully sought (Luke 10:38-42).

One is never to neglect spiritual preparation—not even for the joy of serving others. On the other hand, spiritual preparation will motivate us to serve others. The "one thing" Martha needed was in addition to, not in place of, what she was already doing.

The best way to make homemaking a joyous task is to offer it as unto the Lord; the only way to avoid the drudgery in such mundane work is to bathe the tasks with prayer and catch a vision of the divine challenge in making a home, helping a husband, and nurturing a child. Brother Lawrence, a member of the barefoot Carmelite monks in Paris in the 1600s, set a worthy example:

> Lord of all pots and pans and things. . . . Make me a saint by getting meals and washing up the plates! . . . The time of business does not with me differ from the time of prayer, and in the noise and clatter of my kitchen . . . I possess God in as great tranquillity as if I were upon my knees at the blessed sacrament.[7]

Many people are surprised to discover how much time it actually takes to run a household and care for a family. Having a marketplace career was far easier for me than being a homemaker! None of my former professional positions required my being on the job twenty-four hours every day. None of my varied career pursuits demanded such a variety of skills and abilities as I have exercised in homemaking responsibilities. Automatic, labor-saving devices eliminate much physical work, but increased mobility and multiplied outside activities add to the overall time demands so that the preparation and care of the family shelter are important enough for God Himself to make the assignment for that responsibility.

Of course, much of the world would agree that being a housekeeper is acceptable as long as you are not caring for your own home; treating men with attentive devotion would also be all right as long as the man is the boss in the office and not your husband; caring for children would even be deemed heroic service for which presidential awards could be given as long as the children are someone else's and not your own. You must not be overcome by the surrogacy of this age, which offers even a sub-

stitute womb for those so encumbered by lofty pursuits that they
cannot accept God-given roles and assignments.

HOMEMAKING—A SOURCE OF SELF-ESTEEM

Women join men in the search for accomplishments and positive
evaluations. Every human being has an innate desire to have
worth. God's ideal woman has such worth. In fact, her worth cannot be fixed or estimated—it is "far more precious than jewels"
(Prov. 31:10). The question, of course, is clear: Who has such
worth? The Hebrew word *chayil*, translated "virtuous" but more
literally "strength,"[8] is found also in Proverbs 12:4 and 31:29 as
well as in Ruth 3:11. The word is further translated as "activity,
ability, valor, wealth, efficiency, endurance, capability, energy."
This "woman of strength" enjoys dignity and importance in the
administrative affairs of her home. She is a valuable helpmeet for
her husband. She is a complement to him and necessary to complete his being.

There is beautiful reciprocity in this mutual relationship
between husband and wife, just as there is between Christ and
the church. Christ is the head of the church, and the church is
delighted to serve Him (Eph. 5:23; Phil. 3:7-8). Christ finds joy
in the church, and the church finds in Christ an inheritance of
untold value. This husband has confidence in his wife's ability as
the manager of the household affairs. She is absolutely depend-
able. The gain that accrues to her husband from her thrift and
industry assures that he "will have no lack of gain" (Prov. 31:11).
This "woman of strength" is a visionary investor. With her sav-
ings or inheritance or investment money given to her by her husband, "She considers a field and buys it" (Prov. 31:16). Unlike the
unfaithful servant who hid the talent given to him by his master
(Matt. 25:24-25), this prudent wife is continually adding to her

husband's investments, which is confirmed when "she plants a vineyard" on the field she has purchased (Prov. 31:16).

The woman of strength is an elegant lady. The use of tapestry for bedding, carpeting, and pillows was a sign of a carefully decorated home interior. Silk cloth had not yet been invented, but she undoubtedly used the fine flax or linen cloth that was the best fabric of the day. Her garments were purple, indicating wealth or high rank, and rare indeed (Prov. 31:22). God's woman does give time and effort to her appearance.

These words were written about the wife of the great eighteenth-century preacher Jonathan Edwards:

> But Sarah's husband made it clear that he treasured her as more than a housekeeping drudge and the mother of extra farmhands. So she stayed attractive, and fifteen years later she was still able to entrance men much younger than she was.[9]

The "woman of strength" was a source of tremendous pride to her husband. Her complete management of the household freed her husband to concentrate on his labors. Her husband respected her for neatness of dress and appreciated the fact that his wife was held in high esteem. She was willing to ". . . let her works praise her in the gates" (Prov. 31:31), but there is no hint in the passage that she had any other purpose than to meet the needs of her family in the best possible way.

QUESTIONS FOR REVIEW AND CONTEMPLATION

1. What training and preparation have equipped you to be a homemaker?
2. What character traits do you have or are you working on to enhance your effectiveness as a homemaker?

3. What is your definition of a homemaker?
4. What did you learn about biblical guidelines for homemaking from Proverbs 31?
5. Record your own goals for managing your household more effectively.

SCRIPTURES TO STUDY

Proverbs 31:1-31; Titus 2:3-5

A LOOK AT THE PROVERBS 31 WOMAN OF STRENGTH

- woman with a heart sensitive to God (v. 10)
- woman committed to her husband (v. 11)
- woman determined to keep the home (v. 12)
- willing worker (vv. 13-14)
- priority planner (v. 15)
- visionary investor (v. 16)
- prepared watch-woman (v. 17)
- creative counterpart (vv. 18-19)
- generous benefactor (v. 20)
- protective mother (v. 21)
- elegant lady (v. 22)
- conduit of usefulness (vv. 23-24)
- instrument of optimism (v. 25)
- channel of kindness (v. 26)
- example of faithfulness (v. 27)
- receiving reaper (v. 28)
- bearer of the promise of excellence (v. 29)
- woman marked by the priority of obedience (v. 30)
- recipient of the prize of bearing fruit (v. 31)

3

Is Being a Wife a Fulfilling Function?

The wife was created by God to be her husband's "helper" (*'ezer kenegdo*, Hebrew, "a help like or corresponding to himself," Gen. 2:18). There is nothing demeaning about being a helper. It is a challenging and rewarding responsibility. God Himself assumed that role on many occasions (Ps. 40:17, "You are my help and my deliverer; do not delay, O my God"; Heb. 13:6, "So we can confidently say, 'The Lord is my helper'"). This terminology does not suggest that the Lord was an inferior being but spoke rather of His desire to meet the needs of those whom He loves with an everlasting and unconditional love. Through the ages some have held that women are inferior to men, but the attempt to attribute such an idea to Scripture is unthinkable.

Every believer must give attention to what Luther called "the plain sense of Scripture" as concerns the husband-wife relationship. It is really not terribly complicated. What the New Testament writers wrote and how they meant their words to be understood in their own time is far more important than the secular meanings assigned these biblical terms in this generation, especially when those meanings depart from the clear teaching of Scripture. The fact is that there is no suggestion in Scripture that women in any sense are inferior or incapable—neither in personhood, which is the same as man's, nor in function, which is different from man's. Both the man and the woman are created in God's image, but each has an assignment from God (Gen. 1:27; 2:15-18).

Any attitude or action suggesting a woman's insignificance, inferiority, or lack of personhood originated in the Fall. The stigma of inferiority is no more appropriate for the wife than it would be for Christ. You can be subject to a superior, as Israel was subject to the Lord (Deut. 6:1-5) and as believers are subject to Christ (Phil. 2:9-11) or as Abraham submitted to the priesthood of Melchizedek (Heb. 7:7).

But subordination is also possible among equals: Christ is equal to God the Father and yet subject to Him (Phil. 2:6-8); believers are equal to one another and yet are admonished to submit "to one another out of reverence for Christ" (Eph. 5:21). In fact, you can be called to subordinate yourself to someone who is inferior, as Christ submitted to Pontius Pilate, making "no answer, not even to a single charge" (Matt. 27:11-14).

The mere fact that wives are told to be subject to their husbands tells nothing about their status. It is the comparison of the relationship between husband and wife to the relationship of God the Father with God the Son that settles the matter of status forever.[10]

Submission and authority, which to the feminists are the offensive elements associated with biblical womanhood, are not terms that in themselves connote sinful or evil characteristics. The terms submission and authority do not refer only to role relationships between the sexes. Both terms are used to describe relationships within the family, including, but not exclusive to, the relationship between husband and wife.

In fact, these terms even reach far beyond the family. In every facet of organized society (see Rom. 13:1-5 for application to government and Heb. 13:17 as concerns the church), there must be both authority and submission to authority; otherwise there is anarchy. There simply is no justification for labeling these words and the concepts they embody as innately objectionable and oppressive. Finally and more importantly, these terms point to the believer's common ground with the Lord Himself, who gave to us the highest example of servanthood, obedience, and selflessness as "he humbled himself by becoming obedient to the point of death" (Phil. 2:5-8; see also John 5:30).

Ideally, the care of one's partner is inherent in marriage. Each makes an active and unique (not passive and the same) contribution to the marriage, and each depends upon the other for that contribution. Both husband and wife achieve their respective individuality by assuming different roles, for which each is needed and on which neither intrudes. In choosing to allow her husband to support the family, a wife can turn her ingenuity toward producing a lifestyle even better than an additional salary would buy.

Subordination has been distorted before in the history of the church. Arius assigned inferiority of being to Jesus the Son, refusing to accept the Scripture's statement that Father, Son, and Holy Spirit are equal in being and personhood (John 1:1; 5:23; 10:30; 14:6-7, 9, 11) and yet different in office and function. The Son voluntarily becomes subject to and subordinate[11] to the Father (John 5:19-20; 6:38; 8:28-29, 54; 1 Cor. 15:28; Phil. 2:5-11), and the Holy Spirit is sent by, and thus under the direction of, the Father to glorify the Son (John 14:26; 15:26; 16:13-14).

Arian subordinationism was condemned as heretical—a denial of Trinitarianism—because it ignored, distorted, or misread certain Scriptures and simply dismissed or abandoned passages that the human mind could not explain (a view called Gnosticism).[12] Can "Arian" feminism—which denies that women can have equal personhood along with a subordinate role, i.e., a different role with equal worth—be any more circumspect? I certainly think not. The Council of Nicea in A.D. 325 not only condemned this heresy but also ascribed to both the Son and the Spirit an equality of being, while clearly declaring subordination of order and function.[13] Likewise, I have no problem in accepting within my womanhood the equality of creation and personhood, while recognizing that my divinely bestowed womanhood is uniquely suited to the task divinely assigned to me by the Creator God.

Too many women rush headlong into a career outside the home, determined to waste no time or effort on housework or baby-sitting but rather seeking to achieve position and means by directing all talents and energies toward professional pursuits, which society deems more important and fulfilling. Many "perfect jobs" may indeed come and go during a woman's childrearing years, but only one will absolutely never come along again—the job of rearing your own children and allowing them what has become the increasingly rare opportunity to grow up at home under the direct and constant supervision of their own mother. She awakens them in the morning, serves breakfast, and gets them off for the day. She is on call and available during the day to retrieve a forgotten paper, to rescue and nurse to health when an unexpected fever comes, to drive for a class excursion. She is waiting for a joyous homecoming with snacks and a listening ear. She supervises homework and play, prepares and presides over the dinner hour. She goes through bedtime rituals and oversees preparation for the coming day.

Golda Meir, a former prime minister of Israel, by her own testimony, devoted her adult life to the birth and rearing of Israel at the cost of her marriage. She separated from her reticent husband in her pursuit of public life. To quote Mrs. Meir: "What I was made it impossible for him to have the sort of wife he wanted and needed. . . . I had to decide which came first: my duty to my husband, my home and my child or the kind of life I myself really wanted. Not for the first time—and certainly not for the last—I realized that in a conflict between my duty and my innermost desires, it was my duty [to professional pursuits] that had the prior claim."[14]

How sad for a woman to try to build her life on the notion that she is going to pursue whatever momentarily happens to gratify her needs socially, emotionally, physically, or professionally. Although the duties of wife and mother may lay claim, the Lord warned that the desires of personal ambition and success in public or professional service can take hold:

> But each person is tempted when he is lured and enticed by his own desire [*epithumia*, Greek, expressing the idea of intense desire without restraint, usually culminating in passionate pursuit of something outside the will of God]. Then desire when it has conceived gives birth to sin [*hamartia*, Greek, "missing the mark"], and sin when it is fully grown brings forth death. (James 1:14-15)

When a wife goes to work outside the home, often her husband and children go through culture shock. Suddenly the husband has added to his vocational work increased family assignments. He is frustrated over the additional work, guilty over his wife's increased fatigue, and frustrated by the extended hours necessary to keep up at home. God did personally give the husband the responsibility of providing for the family (Gen. 2:15; 1 Tim. 5:8). To sabotage his meeting that responsibility is often a debilitating blow to the husband as well as a burden to the marriage.

A woman's career can easily serve as a surrogate husband since during employment hours she is ruled by her employer's preferences. Because the wife loses much of her flexibility with the receipt of a paycheck, a husband must bend and adapt his schedule for emergencies with the children, visits to the home by repairmen, etc. Then two employers are left without totally committed employees, and children lose a primary caretaker utterly devoted to their personal needs and nurturing. Note the prophet's warning: "My people—infants are their oppressors, and women rule over them. O my people, your guides mislead you and they have swallowed up the course of your paths" (Isa. 3:12).

Many women still see the paycheck as an inadequate trade for the sights and sounds and tastes of home. Although to some, paychecks represent independence and achievement, to be bound to paychecks requires in exchange the time formerly allotted to work for the family in private, personal ways.

My plea to women to consider the overwhelming importance of giving full energies to home and family is not to say that there are never times when a woman should seek employment outside her home. Nevertheless, the day is coming when a woman's employment outside the home is the rule rather than the exception, leaving too many vacancies in the job of guarding the hearth. Seemingly too many families have no one giving primary attention to the home and to nurturing the next generation.

The most outstanding ministry couple in the New Testament is the dynamic duo Aquila and Priscilla, who traveled the apostolic world together, sharing the gospel of Christ and expounding the Word more fully (Acts 18:2-3, 18, 26). Priscilla must have been a diligent and discerning student of the Word of God, or she could never have impressed the learned Apollos. On the other hand, she must have been a gracious hostess to have endeared her home and hospitality to Paul. Obviously, she was encouraged to take an active part in ministry by her husband. When a godly wife is all she ought to be, she completes, complements, and extends her husband. Their joint ministry reaches beyond what either of them could do alone (Ps. 34:3; Eccl. 4:9-12).

When Paige Patterson invited me to link my life to his, irrevocably and inseparably, he asked me to join him in study and preparation. How grateful I have been for the formal studies of seminary, but how much more grateful I am for the hours Paige has spent as my teacher and mentor. Paige has encouraged me in multifarious ministry, but never has he given me the impression that these ministries were to be more important than keeping our home and rearing our children.

QUESTIONS FOR REVIEW AND CONTEMPLATION

1. What are your thoughts about the role of a "helper"—a position of honor or a role of servitude?
2. How do you feel about biblical submission? According to Scripture, is it a mandate of God or a device of man?
3. Does the Bible advocate authority structures? If so, what are the authorities in your life?
4. Study the verses from Scripture concerning the equality of being and the difference of role found within the Godhead. Why is this study important to you?
5. Examine your own beliefs in light of the personal priorities God has given you. Are there changes you need to make?

BEING A HELPER MEANS:

You as a wife become a full partner with your husband in the overwhelming task of obeying God through having dominion over the earth and continuing the generations (Gen. 1:28).

BEING SUBMISSIVE MEANS:

Submission is more than obedience; it is resting, leaning, trusting, abandoning yourself to another. Submission is more than action; it is an attitude of the will that bends, and willingly so, seeking ways to obey. It is devoid of stubbornness. It begins inside with the will but works outward with purpose. Submission is based upon the confidence that God's way is best. It acknowledges how awesome and capable God is rather than dwelling on how burdensome your husband is. Submission should not be based on what kind of husband you have but on what kind of God you serve.[15]

4

Is Being a Mother a
Worthy Service?

In Scripture godly women were not concerned with whether or not they would receive discrimination in the marketplace but rather with whether or not their wombs were barren. Women were not pining away, pleading with the Almighty that they might be priests or prophets. They were praying for the privilege of bearing a child. In Israel every Jewish mother hoped to become the mother of the Messiah, whose coming had been promised to Eve, the first mother (Gen. 3:15).

Hannah was brokenhearted over her childlessness (1 Sam. 1:1—2:1). Feeling forsaken of God, she was prompted by her maternal instinct to agonizing prayer for a child, with her heart's burning intent to give the boy back to God as a living sacrifice. Hannah deemed nurturing a child the highest service. This motivation was not borne out of slavery to procreative responsibility. She was a brilliant and spiritually sensitive woman, as is shown in her poetic psalm (1 Sam. 2:1-10). In conversations with her husband and Eli the priest, she was treated as an equal (1 Sam. 1:21-23). The decision of when to go to Shiloh was left entirely with Hannah (1 Sam. 1:23), and she not only was given the privilege of announcing the name of the child, but she also apparently chose the name Samuel, saying, "I have asked for him from the LORD" (1 Sam. 1:20, 22). Hannah was her own woman, but for her this meant committing herself to the purposes of God, and she knew no higher purpose than being a wife and mother.

Hannah went from brokenhearted barrenness to extraordinarily privileged maternity. Although Hannah's psalm of thanksgiving marked her as a poetess and prophetess with a spiritual lyric equal to any psalm and full of theological truth, and although her words became the basis for Mary's Magnificat (Luke 1:46-55), Hannah did not reckon her literary acclaim equal to the task of nurturing her child. Her greatest reward was not the birth of a son, however, but giving to God that son, who perhaps beyond all men had power with and from God (1 Sam. 1:27; 3:19-20). Moments of unequaled joy are coupled with difficult and time-consuming work. Children are not things to be acquired, used according to your time and schedule, showcased for your personal satisfaction, and then put aside to facilitate convenience and personal ambition.

Rearing the next generation is a coveted task despite the unprecedented attacks in this generation on motherhood. Some women want to limit parenthood to the labor room, settling for a "maternity sabbatical" in which they birth a baby during a few weeks' leave before rushing back to their lofty pursuits. Mrs. Uyterlinde returned to her job as an executive secretary at an insurance company four months after the birth of her triplets, saying, "I could only do that with the help of two full-time housekeepers." She continued, "Working is easier than being at home, but I give them my total attention when I am at home. Luckily, they don't all want it at the same time."[16]

Other mothers opt to take parenthood a bit more seriously and thus choose the "mommy track" work plan so that their hours have some flexibility while the children are very young.[17] Still others depict motherhood as an awful condition, suffocating and degrading—psychic suicide. Their banner is "Motherhood—Just Say No!" God's warning through the prophet Ezekiel could not be more timely:

> And you took your sons and your daughters, whom you had borne to me, and these you sacrificed to them to be devoured. Were your whorings so small a matter? . . . Behold, everyone who uses proverbs will use this proverb about you: "Like mother, like daughter." You are the daughter of your mother, who loathed her husband and her children; and you are the sister of your sisters, who loathed their husbands and their children. (Ezek. 16:20, 44-45)

Motherhood is both a demanding and a rewarding profession. Unfortunately, the reward often comes much later in life. Nevertheless, a prime characteristic of the good mother is unselfishness; she can wait for the final realization of her rewards. No one—not teacher, preacher, or psychologist—has the same opportunity to mold minds, nurture bodies, and develop potential usefulness. That the woman who bears and nurses the baby should care for the young and for the dwelling in which the young live is both practical and consistent with the basic qualities that nature has given male and female.

Although a woman living in the twenty-first century is different in many ways from her foremothers, she is in at least one way forever the same. Some would say that she is a servant of her biological fate, to which she has to adjust her other pursuits. Of course, this condition may be interpreted as mere slavery with the procreative and nurturing tasks as the shackles; but, on the other hand, this biological duty may also be accepted as a divinely assigned destiny with the awesome opportunity for a woman to link hand and heart with the Creator God as the binding cord in bearing and preparing the next generation.

Despite pressures and difficulties, the job can be overwhelmingly satisfying and amazingly productive because the result of really competent mothering will be passed from generation to generation. Products in the marketplace may come and go, but generation after generation mothers produce their sons and daughters. A child needs his mother to be all there—to be focused on him, to recognize his problems and needs; to support, guide, see, listen to him, love, and want him. A young woman wrote to "Dear Abby," describing her mother as "a professional woman who collected a husband, a daughter, and a dog to enrich her life." According to the daughter, the only one not damaged by this enrichment was the dog![18]

Susanna Wesley, the incomparably brilliant and well-educated mother of sons who shook two continents for Christ, wrote, "I am content to fill a little space if God be glorified." She described her now famous principles for childrearing with this commitment:

> No one can, without renouncing the world, in the most literal sense, observe my method; and there are few, if any, that would entirely devote above twenty years of the prime of life in hopes to save the souls of their children, which they think may be saved without so much ado; for that was my principal intention, however unskillfully and unsuccessfully managed.[19]

The emergence of inexpensive, effective birth-control measures, not to mention widespread abortion, has cut the size of average families. Women are giving less and less of their time to childbearing and rearing; marriage is being delayed to allow career preparation and pursuit. Motherhood has become as mechanical and insignificant as any other household task and is just as quickly farmed out to others—even to the carrying of the child in the womb, i.e., surrogate childbearing through in vitro fertilization.

Marriage has become such a partnership that the household tasks are carefully divided and assigned as nonchalantly as clients to be serviced. Both husband and wife choose careers according to the best earning power and opportunity for advancement of both, which usually means the family loses the best opportunity for both. Despite all this egalitarian emphasis, Mary Jo Bane of the Wellesley Women's Research Center expressed a prevailing sentiment: "Everybody is in favor of equal pay, but nobody is in favor of doing the dishes."[20]

Feminism is a "social movement" that demands it all. Actress Katharine Hepburn said in an interview:

> I'm not sure any woman can successfully pursue a career and be a mother at the same time. The trouble with women today is that they want everything. But no one can have it all. I haven't been handicapped by children. Nor have I handicapped children by bringing them into the world and going ahead with my career.[21]

Actress Joanne Woodward says, "My career has suffered because of the children, and my children have suffered because of my career. I've been torn and haven't been able to function fully

in either arena. I don't know one person who does both success-
fully, and I know a lot of working mothers."[22] Golda Meir con-
fessed that she suffered nagging doubts about the price her two
children paid for her career, adding, "You can get used to any-
thing if you have to, even to feeling perpetually guilty."[23]

These interviews were shocking when they were first introduced. Most women in the 1970s and 1980s were still committed homemakers. In the modern era, no one is surprised; most
are immune from family responsibilities. Some women would
say, "We've come a long way, baby!" The question becomes:
Where are we—the wives and mothers? And more important,
where are they—our husbands and children? More crime, more
drugs, more promiscuity, more divorce. Could there be any con-
nection between the upward spiral of wives and mothers to lofty
pursuits beyond the home and the downward spiral in the state
of the family and the nation?

Each of these women chose to work, not because she had to
do so to provide necessities for her family or because her husband
demanded it, but because of personal gain and fame or because
of what she perceived to be a contribution more valuable to the
nation or world than full-time motherhood. In each case, attention to the child by default became less important than the
career.

Even the politicians are convinced that children are a valuable resource to be protected. A report released by the National
Governors' Association Task Force on Children stated, "The eco-
nomic and social well-being of the United States rests on our ability to assure that our children develop into healthy,
well-educated, and productive citizens. . . . To invest in their
future is to invest in ours."[24]

A study of primarily middle-class children was conducted by

University of Texas at Dallas researchers Deborah Lowe Vandell and Mary Anne Corasaniti. This study indicated that full-time childcare was associated with poorer study skills, lower grades, diminished self-esteem, and inadequate social interaction. Those children who went into full-time care after the first year did not develop as well socially, emotionally, and intellectually as those in part-time care or those whose mothers stayed home with them.

Surely another concern must be in the development of the child's values and worldview, which are determined very early in life. Will forty hours a week in a daycare center be a more formidable factor in forming those values than a worn-out mother? Because Vandell is a full-time professor and mother of three- and eight-year-old children, she had expected different results from the study. She clearly stated that she did not accept her findings as a call for mothers to stay at home.[25] Nevertheless, the findings speak for themselves.

Napoleon was asked what could be done to restore the prestige of France. He replied, "Give us better mothers!"[26] The art of mothering surely demands as much training as a skilled waitress or craft worker, and thus you should not expect to be an expert mother as you begin this vocation. Rather slowly you will learn the needs of each child and how to meet those needs. Often those who are reluctant to begin the job of full-time mothering are just as reluctant to give it up when the results are both seen and enjoyed. Timothy Dwight, former president of Yale, said, "All that I am and all that I shall be I owe to my mother."[27] Good lives don't just grow like Topsy; they are built by people who care.

Isn't it amazing that legislators are looking for ways to enable families to send their children to daycare rather than looking for ways to enable mothers to stay at home with their children?

Megan Rosenfeld comments, "For the first time it is possible to envision a generation that will have spent the bulk of their childhood in an institution."[28] Sad but true is the fact that institutions are now set up to provide a substitute for the mother, who was the moral backbone and spiritual nurturer as well as the physical caretaker—the woman who is now no longer there!

Tatyana Zaslavskaya, when president of the Soviet Sociologist Association, was quoted in a TASS interview as expressing deep concern for the ill effects on children of "the high rate of employment among working-age women." She pleaded for mothers to make children their prime mission, calling on the Communist Party to discuss ways to reduce the employment rate among mothers. She added that the problem that is often glamorized in the United States as the "Superwoman" phenomenon (the woman who is faster than a speeding two-year-old, able to leap tall laundry piles in a single bound, and possessed of more power than three teenaged boys and still able to go out and save the world in the midst of it all) has been known in the Soviet Union for years as "the problem of two jobs."[29] Even Mikhail Gorbachev, while premier of the Soviet Union, addressed this issue:

> We have discovered that many of our problems—in children's and young people's behavior, in our morals, culture and in production—are partly caused by the weakening of family ties and slack attitude to family responsibilities. This is a paradoxical result of our sincere desire to make women equal with men in everything.

He added that Russia, during his tenure, was looking for ways to make it possible for women to return "to their purely womanly mission."[30] The Soviet Union as such has disintegrated, and communism is no longer a dominant worldview, but mothers today—in this postmodern era—would do well to heed these words and learn a lesson from an empire that has crumbled.

Some women even claim to have a higher focus on serving God—putting the gospel ahead of "familyism."[31] While no one and nothing must come between a woman and her personal relationship to Christ ("But seek first the kingdom of God and his righteousness, and all these things will be added to you," Matt. 6:33), neither does the Bible contain any admonition to place the work of the church ahead of home responsibilities. When a woman has chosen the high calling of being a wife, her submission to her husband is "as to the Lord" (Eph. 5:22). When she accepts the high calling of motherhood ("Behold, children are a heritage from the LORD, the fruit of the womb a reward," Ps. 127:3), this commitment, too, is itself an offering to the Lord.

In another era the beautiful and godly mother of John Chrysostom was widowed at a young age. She refused her many suitors and committed herself totally to the responsibility of rearing her gifted son, who became the greatest orator of the Patristic church.[32] Mothers, too, win most by losing all. "Whoever finds his life will lose it, and whoever loses his life for my sake will find it" (Matt. 10:39). By developing the Christlike quality of abandoning personal demands and rights and seeking to serve and minister to those whom God has appointed for their own personal ministry, these unselfish heroines choose to give themselves, their energies, their creativity, and their passion wholly to the task of mothering. In so doing, they gain worth and wonder and splendor beyond imagination.

There is no greater need for the coming years than a revival of interest in the responsibilities of motherhood. This generation needs mothers who are not just family-oriented but family-obsessed. Much has been said about the virtue of determined childlessness and the right to make your own place in the sun; yet to locate an aging mother who believes she made a mistake in pouring her life into her children will be difficult, and it certainly is nigh to impossible to find a child who will testify that his mother loved him and poured herself into his life to his detriment. Surely countless mothers would join me in saying, "Try it—you'll like it!" The Lord Himself says, "Like arrows in the hand of a warrior are the children of one's youth. Blessed is the man who fills his quiver with them!" (Ps. 127:4-5).

QUESTIONS FOR REVIEW AND CONTEMPLATION

1. Why are children important to women?
2. Discuss maternity as a part of the feminine nature.
3. What does Scripture say about the value of a child?
4. Discuss the demands and rewards of motherhood.
5. Describe a mother you know who has made a difference in the life of her child and in her community.
6. How do other responsibilities interface with tasks in the home?

SCRIPTURES TO STUDY

1 Samuel 1:1—2:11; Psalm 139:1-24

A MOTHER'S TASK

Being a mother is a divinely appointed ministry.
- Mother provides solace and comfort for her children.
- Mother vicariously feels the hurts, experiences, and joys of her children.

- Mother loves her children passionately and unconditionally.
- Mother is God's channel for spiritual nurture, passing on to her children the lovingkindness and tender mercy of her loving heavenly Father.
- Mother shapes and develops—even controls for a time—the personal choices and actions of her children. She, with God's help, is molding the future lives of her children.

Conclusion

Despite the clear positive principles and the precise warnings of consequences for those who ignore or distort God's plan for the home and family, this present world is very "upside-down," as described by the prophet Isaiah:

> You turn things upside down! Shall the potter be regarded as the clay, that the thing made should say of its maker, "He did not make me"; or the thing formed say of him who formed it, "He has no understanding"? (Isa. 29:16)

The efforts of contemporary society to eradicate the differences between the sexes have spawned an increase in strident lesbianism and open homosexuality, a quantum upward leap in divorce, an increase in rapes and sexual crimes of all sorts—and families smaller in size than ever before. The women of this generation have prostituted the creative purposes of God by prophesying "out of their own minds" (Ezek. 13:17); they have erected for themselves "images of men" to supplant the Creator's design (Ezek. 16:17), and they have cast aside the greatest blessing of the Creator, i.e., the fruit of the womb (Ezek. 16:20, 44-45). They have allowed Scripture itself to be distorted so that women are conforming themselves to this age and letting the world squeeze them "into its own mold" (Rom. 12:2, PHILLIPS).

The church today sounds like the world twenty-five years ago; the church has lost its great power to stand against culture. Scripture has been shanghaied to suit the purposes of the age and to conform to the current cultural scene. Virtues and vices have been inverted so that self-gratifying personal rights, selfishness, and self-interests are exalted, whereas self-effacing submission, humility, and service to others are degraded. While I am not implying that every career woman is selfish, I am saying that the social atmosphere that causes women to crave professional pursuits as deserving more of their time and energy and creativity than the family is perverted by unbiblical assumptions and an ungodly spirit of self-assertion and self-gratification.

Evangelical or biblical feminism is in large measure a product of the secular women's liberation movement of the last century (especially the 1960s and 1970s). Few of these evangelical feminists have much in common with the radical wing of feminism. Nevertheless, the movement of self-assertion in the home, church, and community cannot but extend into the spiritual realm, imbuing people with a determination to act independently of God and go their own way (Prov. 14:12; Isa. 53:6). Human rights and reason have been exalted over responsibility and divine revelation. The reality in Scripture has been subordinated to the reason of man (and woman); the absolutes of the Creator have been replaced with the whims of the creation. Rejecting Scripture as authoritative, many male and female feminists put the focus of authority in human hands, usually through some hermeneutical casuistry (i.e., distortions and revisionism in interpreting Scripture). Texts that do not seem to affirm women's desire to do as they please are labeled as not authoritative, while texts judged as affirming this desire are authoritative.

There is great resistance in the world of feminism to letting Scripture speak for itself. Instead of coming reverently to the biblical text to see what God says and then declaring themselves to be feminists, many seem to have found something in secular feminism and in its claims for improving the lot of womanhood that seemed good and true to them. Thus, the feminists took a "leap of faith" to attach themselves to this movement, determining to legitimize their position biblically and theologically and to change two millennia of church history and tradition to reflect this new church doctrine. The feminist position more nearly fits the reality of their active professional lives—another tragic example of the world's setting the agenda for the church rather than vice versa.

Homemaking—if pursued with energy, imagination, and skills—has as much challenge and opportunity, success and failure, growth and expansion, perks and incentives as any corporation, plus something no other position offers—working for people you love most and want to please the most!

In the words of Scripture I have found a worthy challenge:

> You shall teach them to your children, talking of them when you are sitting in your house, and when you are walking by the way, and when you lie down, and when you rise . . . that your days and the days of your children may be multiplied in the land that the LORD swore to your fathers to give them, as long as the heavens are above the earth. (Deut. 11:19, 21)

Homemaking—being a full-time wife and mother—is not a destructive drought of uselessness but an overflowing oasis of opportunity; it is not a dreary cell to contain your talents and skills but a brilliant catalyst to channel creativity and energies into meaningful work; it is not a rope for binding your productivity in the marketplace, but reins for guiding your posterity in the home; it is not oppressive restraint of intellectual prowess for the community, but a release of wise instruction to your own household; it is not the bitter assignment of inferiority to your person, but the bright assurance of the ingenuity of God's plan for complementarity of the sexes, especially as worked out in God's plan for marriage; it is neither limitation of gifts available nor stinginess in distributing the benefits of those gifts, but rather the multiplication of a mother's legacy to the generations to come and the generous bestowal of all God meant a mother to give to those He entrusted to her care.

QUESTIONS FOR REVIEW AND CONTEMPLATION

1. How has the modern world been turned "upside-down" as concerns women?
2. How has "evangelical" or "biblical" feminism affected the home and church?
3. Evaluate your role as homemaker, wife, and mother. Are you on target with biblical patterns? Do you have changes to make?

Appendix
The Danvers Statement

The "Danvers Statement" summarizes the need for the Council on Biblical Manhood and Womanhood (CBMW) and serves as an overview of our core beliefs. This statement was prepared by several evangelical leaders at a CBMW meeting in Danvers, Massachusetts, in December of 1987.* It was first published in final form by the CBMW in Wheaton, Illinois, in November of 1988.

RATIONALE

We have been moved in our purpose by the following contemporary developments, which we observe with deep concern:

1. The widespread uncertainty and confusion in our culture regarding the complementary differences between masculinity and femininity;

2. The tragic effects of this confusion in unraveling the fabric of marriage woven by God out of the beautiful and diverse strands of manhood and womanhood;

3. The increasing promotion given to feminist egalitarianism

with accompanying distortions or neglect of the glad harmony portrayed in Scripture between the loving, humble leadership of redeemed husbands and the intelligent, willing support of that leadership by redeemed wives;

4. The widespread ambivalence regarding the values of motherhood, vocational homemaking, and the many ministries historically performed by women;

5. The growing claims of legitimacy for sexual relationships which have biblically and historically been considered illicit or perverse, and the increase in pornographic portrayal of human sexuality;

6. The upsurge of physical and emotional abuse in the family;

7. The emergence of roles for men and women in church leadership that do not conform to biblical teaching but backfire in the crippling of biblically faithful witness;

8. The increasing prevalence and acceptance of hermeneutical oddities devised to reinterpret apparently plain meanings of biblical texts;

9. The consequent threat to biblical authority as the clarity of Scripture is jeopardized and the accessibility of its meaning to ordinary people is withdrawn into the restricted realm of technical ingenuity;

10. And behind all this the apparent accommodation of some within the church to the spirit of the age at the expense of winsome, radical biblical authenticity which in the power of the Holy Spirit may reform rather than reflect our ailing culture.

THE TEN AFFIRMATIONS OF THE DANVERS STATEMENT

Based on our understanding of biblical teachings, we affirm the following:

1. Both Adam and Eve were created in God's image, equal before God as persons and distinct in their manhood and womanhood.

2. Distinctions in masculine and feminine roles are ordained by God as part of the created order, and should find an echo in every human heart.

3. Adam's headship in marriage was established by God before the Fall and was not a result of sin.

4. The Fall introduced distortions into the relationships between men and women.

   * In the home, the husband's loving, humble headship tends to be replaced by domination or passivity; the wife's intelligent, willing submission tends to be replaced by usurpation or servility.

   * In the church, sin inclines men toward a worldly love of power or an abdication of spiritual responsibility, and inclines women to resist limitations on their roles or to neglect the use of their gifts in appropriate ministries.

5. The Old Testament, as well as the New Testament, manifests the equally high value and dignity which God attached to the roles of both men and women. Both Old and New Testaments also affirm the principle of male headship in the family and in the covenant community.

6. Redemption in Christ aims at removing the distortions introduced by the curse.

   * In the family, husbands should forsake harsh or selfish leadership and grow in love and care for their wives; wives should forsake resistance to their husbands' authority and grow in willing, joyful submission to their husbands' leadership.

   * In the church, redemption in Christ gives men and women an equal share in the blessings of salvation; nevertheless,

some governing and teaching roles within the church are restricted to men.

7. In all of life Christ is the supreme authority and guide for men and women, so that no earthly submission—domestic, religious, or civil—ever implies a mandate to follow a human authority into sin.

8. In both men and women a heartfelt sense of call to ministry should never be used to set aside biblical criteria for particular ministries. Rather, biblical teaching should remain the authority for testing our subjective discernment of God's will.

9. With half the world's population outside the reach of indigenous evangelism; with countless other lost people in those societies that have heard the gospel; with the stresses and miseries of sickness, malnutrition, homelessness, illiteracy, ignorance, aging, addiction, crime, incarceration, neuroses, and loneliness, no man or woman who feels a passion from God to make His grace known in word and deed need ever live without a fulfilling ministry for the glory of Christ and the good of this fallen world.

10. We are convinced that a denial or neglect of these principles will lead to increasingly destructive consequences in our families, our churches, and the culture at large.

We grant permission and encourage interested persons to use, reproduce, and distribute The Danvers Statement for noncommercial purposes.

---

*Dorothy Kelley Patterson was a founding member of the Council and helped to draft this document.

Notes

1. Unless specified, all Scripture quotations come from the *English Standard Version*.

2. Frank Zepezauer, "The Masks of Feminism," *The Human Life Review*, Fall 1988, p. 31.

3. Dorothy Morrison, "My Turn," *Newsweek*, October 17, 1988, p. 14.

4. Paul Fussell, "What Happened to Mother?" *The Wilson Quarterly*, vol. 12, no. 5 (Winter 1988), p. 154.

5. David W. Moore, "Family, Health Most Important Aspects of Life" (1/3/03) www.gallup.com/poll/releases/pr030103.asp?Version=p (Accessed 1/31/03) The publisher of this site is The Gallup Organization, Lincoln, Neb.

6. Hymen E. Goldin, *The Jewish Woman and Her Home* (New York: Hebrew Publishing Co., n.d.), pp. 130-131.

7. Brother Lawrence, *The Practice of the Presence of God: With Spiritual Maxims* (Old Tappan, N.J.: Fleming H. Revell Company Publishers, 1958), pp. 11-12.

8. Francis Brown, S. R. Driver, and Charles Briggs, *A Hebrew and English Lexicon of the Old Testament* (Oxford: Clarendon Press, 1962), pp. 288-299.

9. Elizabeth Dodds, *Marriage to a Difficult Man* (Philadelphia: Westminster Press, 1976), p. 84.

10. "What Is Christian Marriage?: A Debate between Larry and Nordis Christenson and Berkeley and Alvera Mickelsen," *Transformation*, vol. 5, no. 3 (July/September 1988), p. 3.

11. Defined as "one who stands in order or rank below another." *Webster's Third New International Dictionary* (Springfield, Mass.: G & C Merriam, 1971), p. 2277.

12. "Subordinationism," *Oxford Dictionary of the Christian Church*, ed. F. L. Cross (London: Oxford University Press, 1958), p. 1301.

13. Augustus Hopkins Strong, *Systematic Theology* (Philadelphia: Judson Press, 1960), p. 342.
14. "Books," *Newsweek*, November 3, 1975, p. 88.
15. Dorothy Kelley Patterson, *The Family: Unchanging Principles for Changing Times* (Nashville, Tenn.: Broadman & Holman Publishers, 2002), p. 42.
16. *The Dallas Morning News*, September 22, 1981.
17. *The Dallas Morning News,* March 11, 1989.
18. Abigail Van Buren, "Dear Abby," *The Northwest Arkansas Times*, September 28, 1974.
19. Rebecca Lamar Harmon, *Susanna, Mother of the Wesleys* (London: Hodder & Stoughton, 1968), p. 57.
20. *San Francisco Examiner*, December 28, 1977.
21. "An Interview with Kate Hepburn," *Ladies Home Journal*, March 1977, p. 54.
22. "Joanne and Paul," *Ladies Home Journal*, July 1975, p. 62.
23. "Books," *Newsweek*, November 3, 1975, p. 88.
24. Kim A. Lawton, "Politicians Discover Children," *Christianity Today*, March 17, 1989, p. 34.
25. Sandra Evans, "Study Shows Negative Effects of Full-Time Child Care," *Washington Post*, April 23, 1988, p. A10.
26. Victor Wilson, "Book Garners Facts, Fancies about Mom," *Dallas Morning News*, May 13, 1984, p. 10F.
27. Dodds, *Marriage to a Difficult Man*, p. 209.
28. Megan Rosenfeld, *Washington Post*, November 9, 1986.
29. Associated Press, June 11, 1988.
30. Mikhail Gorbachev, "In His Words," *U.S. News & World Report*, November 9, 1987, pp. 70-79.
31. Kristin M. Foster, "Ministry and Motherhood: A Collision of Callings?" *Currents in Theology and Mission*, vol. 16, no. 2 (April 1989), p. 102.
32. W. R. Stephens, *Saint John Chrysostom* (London: John Murray, 1880), pp. 9-12.

Recommended Resources

Abbott, John. *The Mother at Home*. Grace Abounding Ministries, 1984.

Alexander, James W. *Thoughts on Family Worship*. Morgan, Pa.: Soli Deo Gloria Publications, 1990.

Angelo, Bonnie. *First Mothers: The Women Who Shaped the Presidents*. New York: William Morrow, 2000.

Dillow, Linda. *Creative Counterpart*. Nashville, Tenn.: Thomas Nelson, 1977.

Dobson, James. *Love for a Lifetime*. Sisters, Ore.: Questar Publishers, 1993.

_____. *The New Dare to Discipline*. Wheaton, Ill.: Tyndale House, 1992.

_____. *The Strong-Willed Child*. Wheaton, Ill.: Tyndale House, 1985.

Elliot, Elisabeth. *Discipline: The Glad Surrender*. Grand Rapids: Revell, 1992.

_____. *Keep a Quiet Heart*. Ann Arbor, Mich.: Servant Publications, 1995.

_____. *Passion and Purity*. Old Tappan, N.J.: Revell, 1984.

Gullan, Harold I. *Faith of Our Mothers: The Stories of Presidential Mothers from Mary Washington to Barbara Bush*. Grand Rapids: Wm. B. Eerdmans, 2001.

Harley, Willard, Jr. *His Needs, Her Needs*. Grand Rapids: Revell, 1996.

Hibbard, Ann. *Family Celebrations at Birthdays and for Vacations and Other Holidays*. Grand Rapids: Baker Book House, 1996.

_____. *Family Celebrations at Christmas*. Grand Rapids: Baker Book House, 1993.

_____. *Family Celebrations at Easter*. Grand Rapids: Baker Book House, 1994.

_____. *Family Celebrations at Thanksgiving and Alternatives to Halloween*. Grand Rapids: Baker Book House, 1995.

La Leche League. *The Womanly Art of Breastfeeding*. New York: Penguin Books, 1997.

LaHaye, Beverly. *Understanding Your Child's Temperament*. Eugene, Ore.: Harvest House Publishers, 1997.

LaHaye, Tim and Beverly. *The Act of Marriage*. Grand Rapids: Zondervan, 1976.

Lehman, Kevin. *Bringing Up Kids Without Tearing Them Down*. New York: Delacorte Press, 1993.

Meier, Paul D. and Linda Burnett. *The Unwanted Generation: A Guide to Responsible Parenting*. Grand Rapids: Baker Book House, 1980.

Miller, Donna J. and Linda Holland. *Growing Little Woman: Capturing Teachable Moments with Your Daughter*. Chicago: Moody Press, 1997.

Patterson, Dorothy Kelley. *The Family: Unchanging Principles for Changing Times*. Nashville, Tenn.: Broadman, 2001.

_____. *The Woman's Study Bible*. Nashville, Tenn.: Thomas Nelson, 1995.

Piper, John and Wayne Grudem. *Recovering Biblical Manhood and Womanhood*. Wheaton, Ill.: Crossway, 1991.

Schaeffer, Edith. *The Hidden Art of Homemaking*. Wheaton, Ill.: Tyndale House, 1980.

_____. *What Is a Family?* Grand Rapids: Baker Book House, 1975.

Tobias, Cynthia Ulrich. *Every Child Can Succeed*. Colorado Springs, Colo.: Focus on the Family Publishing, 1996.

Trobisch, Ingrid. *The Joy of Being a Woman*. New York: Harper, 1976.

Other Resources

by Dorothy Kelley Patterson

BOOKS

Patterson, Dorothy, asst. ed. *The Baptist Study Bible.* Nashville, Tenn.: Thomas Nelson, 2001.

____. *A Woman Seeking God: Discover God in the Places of Your Life.* Nashville, Tenn.: Broadman, 1992.

____, gen. ed. *The Woman's Study Bible.* Nashville, Tenn.: Thomas Nelson, 1995.

____. *BeAttitudes for Women: Wisdom from Heaven for Life on Earth.* Nashville, Tenn.: Broadman, 2000.

____. *The Family: Unchanging Principles for Changing Times.* Nashville, Tenn.: Broadman, 2001.

____. *A Handbook for Ministers' Wives.* Nashville, Tenn.: Broadman, 2002.

ARTICLES AND PARTS OF BOOKS

____. "Is Being a Mother a Worthy Service?" *Living,* Vol. 13:3, Nevada, Iowa: Lutherans for Life, 14-19.

____. "The Study of Submission." *The Theological Educator,* 13:2, 70-79.

____. "The Universal Spare Part: A Look at the Pastor's Wife."

The Church at the Dawn of the 21ˢᵗ Century: Essays in Honor of W. A. Criswell. Dallas: Criswell Publications, 1989.

_____. "The High Calling of Wife and Mother in Biblical Perspective." *Recovering Biblical Manhood and Womanhood.* J. Piper, et al., eds. Wheaton, Ill.: Crossway, 1991, 364-377, 531-532.

_____. "Family Values in Baptist Life." *Baptists Why and Why Not Revisited.* Timothy George and Richard Land, eds. Nashville, Tenn.: Broadman, 1998.

_____. "Nurturing Mothers." *Biblical Womanhood in the Home.* Nancy Leigh DeMoss, ed. Wheaton, Ill.: Crossway, 2002.

_____. *Devotions for Ministry Wives: Encouragement from Those Who've Been There.* Barbara Hughes, ed. Grand Rapids: Zondervan, 2002.

Index

Scripture Index